DATE DUE

MAR 20 1997	
SEP 1 8 1997	
NOV 0 3 1997	
FEB 0 3 1998	
FEB 0 6 1998	
FEB 1 0 1998	
FEB 2 3 1998	
APR 1 7 1998	
11-20-14	

BUSINESS
MEXICO

A Practical Guide to Understanding Mexican Business Culture

Peggy Kenna   **Sondra Lacy**

Printed on recyclable paper

PASSPORT BOOKS
a division of *NTC Publishing Group*
Lincolnwood, Illinois USA

Library of Congress Cataloging-in-Publication Data

Kenna, Peggy.
    Business Mexico: a practical guide to understanding Mexican business
culture / Peggy Kenna, Sondra Lacy.
        p.   cm.
    ISBN 0-8442-3551-2
    1. Business etiquette—Mexico.   2. Corporate culture—Mexico.
    3. Business communication—Mexico.   4. Negotiation in business—
    Mexico.   I. Lacy, Sondra.   II. Title.
HF5389.K457   1994
395' .52'0972—dc20   93—40565
                                                             CIP

Published by Passport Books, a division of NTC Publishing Group.
4255 West Touhy Avenue, Lincolnwood, (Chicago) Illinois 60646-1975, U.S.A.
©1994 by NTC Publishing Group. All rights reserved.
No part of this work may be reproduced, stored in a retrieval system
or transmitted in any form or by any means,
electronic or mechanical, including photocopying and recording or otherwise
without the prior permission of NTC Publishing Group.
Manufactured in the United States of America.

4 5 6 7 8 9 0 VP 9 8 7 6 5 4 3 2 1

Contents

Welcome to Business Mexico   1
The Global Marketplace   3
Doing Business in a Global Market   6
Understanding Mexican Culture   8
    Communication Style   12
    Leadership/Status   18
    Organizational Structure 24
    Punctuality   28
    Meetings   30
    Negotiating   32
U.S. Business Etiquette   38
Mexican Business Etiquette   40
U.S. Gestures   42
Mexican Gestures   43
Communication Interferences   44
Succeeding in International Business   46
Quick Tips: United States   50
Quick Tips: Mexico   51
Common Phrases   54

Peggy Kenna is a communication specialist working with foreign-born employees in the American workplace. She provides cross-cultural training and consultation services to companies conducting business internationally. She is also a certified speech and language pathologist who specializes in accent modification. Peggy lives in Tempe, Arizona.

Sondra Lacy is a certified communications specialist and teaches American communication skills to foreign-born employees in the American workplace. She also provides cross-cultural training and consultation services to companies conducting business internationally. Sondra lives in Scottsdale, Arizona.

Business Mexico is an invaluable tool for thousands of entrepreneurs, businesspeople, corporate executives, technicians, and salespeople seeking to develop lasting business relationships in Mexico.

The book provides a fast, easy way for you to become acquainted with business practices and protocol to help you increase your chances for success in Mexico. You will discover the secrets of doing business internationally while improving your interpersonal communication skills.

Let this book work for you.

> Pam Del Duca
> President/CEO
> The DELSTAR Group
> Scottsdale, Arizona

Entrepreneur Of The Year®
Award Recipient

Business Mexico offers a smooth and problem-free transition between the American and Mexican business cultures.

This pocket-size book contains information you need when traveling in Mexico or doing business with Mexican colleagues. It explains the differences in business culture you will encounter in such areas as:

- Business etiquette

- Communication style

- Problem solving and decision making

- Meetings and presentation style

Business Mexico gets you started on the right track and challenges you to seek ways to improve your success in the global marketplace by understanding cultural differences in the ways people communicate and do business with each other.

Successful international companies are able to adapt to the business styles acceptable in other countries and by other nationalities, based on their knowledge and awareness of key cultural differences. These differences, if not acknowledged and addressed, can interfere in successful communication and can adversely affect the success of any business attempting to expand internationally.

Business Mexico is designed to overcome such difficulties by comparing the American culture with the culture of Mexico. Identifying appropriate behavior in one's own culture can make it easier to adapt to that of the country with which you are doing business. With this in mind, the book's unique parallel layout allows an at-a-glance comparison of Mexican business practices with those of the United States.

Practical and easy to use, *Business Mexico* will help you win the confidence of Mexican associates and achieve common business goals.

The global business environment today is a multicultural one. While general business considerations are essentially the same the world over, business styles differ greatly from country to country. What is customary and appropriate in one country may be considered unusual or even offensive in another. The increasingly competitive environment calls for an individual approach to each national market. The success of your venture outside your home market depends largely upon preparation. The American style of business is not universally accepted. Yet we send our employees, executives, salespeople, technicians to negotiate or carry out contracts with little or no understanding of the cultural differences in the ways people communicate and do business with each other. How many business deals have been lost because of this cultural myopia?

Globalization is a process which is drawing people together from all nations of the world into a single community linked by the vast network of communication technologies. Technological breakthroughs in the past two decades have made instant communication between individuals around the world an affordable reality.

As these technological advances continue to open up and expand the dialogue among members of the world community, the need for effective communication between nations and peoples has accelerated.

When change occurs as dramatically and rapidly as we have witnessed in the past decade, many people throughout the world are being forced to quickly learn and adapt to unfamiliar ways of doing things. Some actually welcome change and the opportunities it presents, while others are reluctant to give up familiar ways of doing things. History proves that cultures are slow to change. But, individuals who are mentally prepared to accept change and deal with differences can successfully adapt to cultures very different from their own.

A culture develops when individuals have common experiences and share their reactions to these experiences by communicating with other members of their society.

Over time, communication becomes the vehicle by which cultural beliefs and values are developed, shared and transmitted from one generation to the next. Communication and culture are mutually dependent.

Effective communication between governments or international businesses requires more than being able to speak the language fluently or relying on expert interpreters. Understanding the language is only the first step. Understanding and accepting the behaviors, customs and attitudes of other cultures while interacting globally is also required to bring harmony and success in the worldwide business and political arena.

The importance of the influence of one's native culture on the way one approaches life cannot be overstated. Each country's cultural beliefs and values are reflected in its people's idea of the "right" way to live and behave.

In general, businesspeople who practice low-key, non-adversarial, win/win techniques in doing business abroad tend to be most successful. Knowing what your company wants to achieve, its bottom line, and also understanding the objectives of the other party and helping to accommodate them in the business transaction are necessary for developing long-term, international business relationships.

Often, representatives from American companies, for example, have difficulty doing business with *each other*, even when they speak the same language and share a common culture. Consider how much more difficult it is to do business with people from different cultures who speak different languages.

Success in the international business arena will not be easy for those who do not take steps to gain the skills necessary to be global players. The language barrier is an obvious problem.

Equally important will be negotiation skills, as well as an understanding of and adaptation to the social and business etiquette of the foreign country. Americans have a reputation for failing to appreciate this. In other words, businesspeople doing business abroad will get off to a good start if they remember to do the following:

- Listen closely; understand the verbal and non-verbal communications.

- Focus on mutual interests, not differences.

- Nurture long-term relationships.

- Emphasize quality. Be prepared to defend the quality of your products and services, and the quality of your business relationship.

The history of Mexico boasts a long line of advanced Indian civilizations, ending with the Aztecs who were conquered by the Spanish in 1519. Mexico gained its independence in 1821. It has a federal government with an executive, legislative, and judicial branch. The president and legislators are chosen by direct elections.

Due largely to the petroleum industry, the economic situation in Mexico has improved a great deal over the last 50 years. Recently, however, Mexico has been in a difficult economic situation with much unemployment and a large foreign debt.

Mexico has been predominantly an agricultural country but its population is largely urban. One-fifth of the population lives in Mexico City. Mining and petroleum production are its most important industries. These industries are now highly developed. Spanish is the national language. Mexico has one of the world's highest population growth rates.

Mexico has been working to modernize and open its markets. Economic reform began in 1982 with the Mexican foreign debt crisis. Mexico has traditionally been very protectionist. The degree of government involvement in business has been extensive but that is changing. Industries such as banking, petroleum, petrochemicals, and aviation have been government owned but in recent years most of these industries are gradually being privatized. Political reform is also coming gradually.

During the mid 1980s when unemployment was low and good low-wage workers were hard to find in the United States, a number of American companies moved to Mexico. Some are now moving back due to the hidden costs of doing business there. Mexico has a very well educated upper class but has had few trained, skilled workers for labor intensive industries. This affects productivity and quality of work.

Unlike Canada, Mexico is not similar to the United States. Mexico has a very different history and cultural tradition. Beginning with the colonization of Mexico by Spain, the country experienced many years of oppression and exploitation. Unlike the United States, Mexico does not have a long tradition of democracy.

In recent years, the influence of American culture has spread in Mexico. However, more traditional values such as family loyalty, personal relationships, and a conservative outlook are still predominant.

The relationship between the United States and Mexico is very sensitive and United States methods and values should not be compared with those of Mexico. Mexican businesspeople don't always want to hear about how things are done in the United States

The American value system assumes that people, apart from social and educational influences, are basically the same. Moreover, Americans believe that each person should be judged on individual merits. These "merits" include a person's worth and character, and they are revealed through the person's actions.

In Mexico, it is the uniqueness of the individual which is valued. Mexicans believe uniqueness is a quality which resides within each person and is not necessarily evident through actions or achievements. This uniqueness, which represents the dignity of each person, must be protected.

Any action or remark that may be interpreted as an intentional slight to the person's dignity is to be considered a serious insult. In addition, every person is part of a larger family grouping and should not be regarded as an isolated individual. Therefore, what is an insult to an individual is also an affront to his or her family.

To Mexicans rank and status are related to personal accomplishments. People in the arts and literature are very highly respected.

In Mexico, the family is very important. Families are large and loyalty to other family members is strong. Mexicans feel they cannot really know a person until they know about their family. Family relationships also involve serious obligations to help each other. Group loyalty is very important. Credibility is established through connections, who you know. The interests of the family are very important.

Remember that within every culture, there are always individual differences among people and organizations. It is also important to remember that Mexico, like many countries is undergoing rapid change.

United States

■ *Direct and to the point*

Americans prefer people who say exactly what they mean, and who are practical, concise and clear. They are suspicious of people who seem unrestrained in their praise and are likely to make light of someone who seems too enamored of titles. Some bragging or boasting is permitted. Americans also tend to minimize differences between people due to sex, age or status.

■ *Masters of our fate*

Americans basically believe they control their own destiny. They believe that all that is necessary is to achieve a goal is to take the initiative and do something.

■ *Indirect*

Mexicans tend to speak in a roundabout way and don't always come to the point. They often enjoy going off on tangents and dislike the American style of "straight" conversation. They may also flatter or attempt to please others to get what they want. They value titles and tend to maximize differences between persons due to sex, status or age. Mexicans value people, and they will speak with pride about their wealth or accomplishments and sometimes may overstate their achievements to impress others.

Mexicans are a warm, friendly and hospitable people who take great delight and pleasure from talk. They value courtesy, diplomacy, dignity and tact.

■ *Deterministic*

Many Mexicans believe in fate and take what comes to them with resignation to the inevitable. Those who take this fatalistic attitude don't feel they have control of their destinies.

Communication Style

United States

■ *Emotion seen as weakness*

Americans believe that emotions have no business at work. They feel that although accuracy is important, errors are tolerated and admitting mistakes is seen as a sign of maturity. Americans believe you learn from failure and therefore encourage risk taking.

Americans also believe disagreements are not to be taken personally and "loss of face" is not a big issue.

■ *Direct eye contact*

Nonverbal cues that a speaker gives are very important to communication in American. Americans believe good listening skills involve keeping eye contact; intermittent eye contact is used when speaking.

■ *Inductive reasoning*

Americans tend to concentrate on the concrete and dislike abstract ideas. They tend to be pragmatic; they value what works and take a practical approach to problem solving.

■ *Loss of face important*

Most Mexicans tend to be very sensitive to differences of opinion. Until they get to know someone, their communication will tend to be indirect. They will proceed cautiously and like to develop a business relationship slowly. Relationships are built on trust. Since failure can cause serious loss of face and dignity, they may tend to avoid taking risks.

■ *Avoid direct eye contact*

To Mexicans, holding the gaze of another person when listening is considered confrontational. They use intermittent eye contact when speaking.

■ *Deductive reasoning*

Mexicans enjoy the intellectual pursuit of abstract concepts. However, they do not always get into the application of these ideas which can affect problem-solving discussions. Mexicans value conformity to group opinion which also affects problem solving and decision making.

United States

■ *Individualism*

Americans have a strong belief in individual rights and believe each individual is responsible personally. Business transactions are more a matter of working out a contract, and personal relationships among the partners involved are less important.

■ *Truth is absolute*

Americans believe that truth is absolute and does not depend on circumstances. A fact is either true or false. They believe that what is true for one person is true for everybody. Americans prefer to use an ambiguous expression such as "it is interesting" rather than tell a lie to someone they don't want to hurt. They also tend to feel that saying nothing is better than telling a lie to make a person feel better.

■ *Personalismo*

Mexicans are concerned about self, family, friends and personal pride. Mexicans like to build relationships before doing business and since they are a male-oriented society at this time, communication should be personalized and addressed to the male. Mexicans like business transactions to be finalized in person, not by phone or letter.

■ *Truth is relative*

Mexicans believe truth should be tempered by diplomacy which may lead to their giving an answer just to please the listener. Mexicans see two kinds of truth: objective and interpersonal. While Americans may say something ambiguous rather than hurt another person, Mexicans intend the same thing but instead may make up an answer or hide the facts. They also don't like to make promises they can't keep. Harmony and dignity of the person are important. This means subordinates may not tell a manager about problems because they don't want to make the manager feel bad. Instead they only give "good news."

United States

■ *Status*

In the United States money is the main status indicator and is the major award for achievement.

■ *Like to debate*

Americans enjoy proving themselves in competitive situations and like to debate issues.

■ *Respect*

To Americans respect includes equality, fair play and the democratic spirit. A manager expects to earn respect through achievements and by building relationships with subordinates.

■ *Status*

To Mexicans, title and position are as important as money. Mexico is a hierarchical society and in general Mexicans accept their station in society. They may even resent North Americans who try to minimize differences and treat people equally. This includes a manager who tries to include subordinates in the decision-making process. They may also resent North Americans who fail to pay proper respect to superiors.

■ *Shun confrontation*

Mexicans tend to avoid personal competition and favor harmony at work. They tend to be very sensitive to criticism.

■ *Respect*

While Mexicans may not like a person in power, they believe in showing proper respect due to that person's age, position or influence. A manager with good technical knowledge is highly respected.

United States

■ *Management style*

American managers are expected to delegate responsibilities and also delegate the authority to carry out those duties. Executives will seek responsibility and also are expected to accept accountability for decisions they make.

■ *Aim for equality*

In many U.S. companies a subtle hierarchy is observed which is determined by personal power, not seniority or status. Employees can easily move up and down within the hierarchy. Americans value fairness. They also like to believe they treat people impartially and without favoritism regardless of sex or race. Bias still exists but it is not admitted.

In the U.S., by law, women must be treated equally with men in the workplace. Women in the U.S. have made significant progress in recent years and are more and more entering management levels is business.

■ *Management style*

Traditional Mexican managers have tended to concentrate power at the top. They have been reluctant to delegate authority. As a result Mexican employees, especially at the lower levels, may assume little or no responsibility for their work because they have been assigned a task and not given authority to carry it out. Mexican workers are hard working and ingenious, but they have felt the need to avoid responsibility for mistakes. This is slowly changing. Many younger managers are starting to delegate responsibility.

■ *Machismo*

Traditionally the male cultural role has included a strong sense of masculinity which stresses courage, virility and authority over women. In business, men are expected to demonstrate forcefulness, self confidence, courage and strong leadership.

Because of this cultural image, very few Mexican women have found their way into management yet, although an increasing number are found in the professions.

United States

■ *Implementation of decisions*

In Americans companies someone is always in charge and there is a clear decision maker. This decision maker can be found at different levels of the organization depending on the importance of the decision. Whoever is put in charge of implementing a decision is expected to be completely accountable for its success or failure.

■ *Implementation of decision*

In Mexico, there is still a belief among many that the boss is all knowing and all powerful. Decisions are made by the one in authority and questioning is not encouraged. This is slowly changing.

One difficulty has been that senior executives have often had trouble passing their knowledge to lower levels of management. When this happens, managers and supervisors may be expected to implement plans they don't fully understand. This can affect their ability to get problems solved and projects completed as expected.

Organizational Structure

United States

■ *Staffing*

In America, the relatives of company officers and managers often are barred from being hired. Favoritism and nepotism are not acceptable, and Americans believe promotions should be based on performance. Generally, employees are motivated to excel at their work by personal ambition.

■ *Planning*

Americans tend to be both strategic and tactical planners. Americans believe it is important to plan for and anticipate the future. Much time and effort is spent in planning concepts and establishing procedures to carry out a plan. Success or failure is dependent on the agreed upon plan. Planning is usually top down but it can be bottom up.

Business contracts are written, detailed and not particularly flexible. Any changes to a contract must be renegotiated. Planning tends to be fairly short-term.

Mexico

■ *Staffing*

In Mexico, family and friends are often favored as employees because they are seen as being trustworthy. Promotions are often based on loyalty to a superior, rather than performance within an organization.

■ *Planning*

Due to an uncertain environment, planning has usually been short-term. In addition, planning tends to be based on the intuition of the chief executive and may not always be communicated effectively throughout the company.

Organizational Structure

United States

■ *Decision making*

Americans expect people to express their opinions openly, and in matters of public policy or group decision making the majority rules. One person, however, is usually given power to make the final decision and bear all responsibility.

Lower level managers often get a chance to provide input. Americans believe that those closest to a problem should have input in determining the solution.

Decisions can be made at all levels of an organization depending on the importance of the decision.

■ *Think big*

Americans usually want to start with a major business transaction, a large contract.

■ *Decision making*

In Mexico decision making is concentrated at the senior levels. Senior level decision makers in Mexico depend on lower level managers to negotiate, analyze and make recommendations.

■ *Start small*

Mexicans like to think in smaller units. They usually like to start a business relationship with a small transaction. Then, as trust is built and the relationship is developed, they will expand their business dealings.

United States

■ *Deadlines/commitments firm*

The United States is very bound by time. Americans tend to put limits on meetings and deadlines on performance. Punctuality is considered very important and it is impolite to be late for a meeting. Schedules are expected to be adhered to.

■ *Fast pace*

Americans want to get down to business right away. They tend to establish relationships quickly and the relationship is usually only temporary until business is completed.

■ *Time is money*

Americans see time as linear and segmented. Once a moment is gone, it is gone forever. Americans talk about "saving time" and "wasting time." And wasting time is like wasting money.

Americans also like to divide the day into segments and schedule each segment. They dislike interruptions.

■ *Deadlines are flexible*

Mexico is the land of "manana," which means tomorrow. If they say something will be done "manana," this means they are not giving you a specific time commitment. If it is important that a specific date be met, this needs to be stressed.

Time is more relative and fluid to Mexicans. Mexicans also tend to do many things at the same time.

■ *Slow pace*

In Mexico the pace of business is slower than in the U.S. Mexicans want to establish relationships first and dislike quick, infrequent visits.

■ *Time is power*

To many Mexicans, being late may be a way of showing the other person that they have no power over you.

Interruptions are common and delays are to be expected.

United States

■ *Impersonal*

Americans like to get right down to business since meetings are usually tightly scheduled and have fixed agendas. They like to spend their time discussing and solving problems and determining action-oriented plans. Americans are not particularly interested in establishing long-term relationships except in a purely business sense.

■ *Presentations*

Americans tend to have a projecting style of presentation. They will often combine informative and persuasive styles as an efficient method of presentation. They attempt to persuade the audience to make a decision or take an action at the same time as they provide information. They consider this an effective and efficient use of time. Americans also believe in the "hard sell" and "quick close" approach to selling. They expect the audience to asked questions and to test the presenter's knowledge. Presenters expect to have to defend their opinions.

Mexico

■ *Establish relationships*

Mexicans like lots of personal conversation. They don't like to get down to business right away. They want to get to know you and feel that they can trust you before they do business. Mexico doesn't really have a meetings culture. They don't like to have too many meetings; the purpose of a meeting is mainly to communicate instructions.

■ *Presentations*

The style of the presentation is as important as its contents to Mexicans. They like persuasiveness and verbal word play and tend to value form as much as substance.

Mexicans appreciate presentations that are forceful, clear, and emphasize stability. They like presentations that center on tangibles. They also like the use of graphs, charts, computer printouts, samples and models.

They generally do not arrive at decisions during or immediately after a presentation.

United States

■ *Task oriented*

Americans are highly task oriented. They are good at taking responsibility and getting things done. They are more interested in the technical aspects of negotiation than in building relationships.

Americans have typically negotiated from a win/lose standpoint. They feel someone wins and someone loses.

■ *Direct and open*

Americans tend to be very direct and open in their communication. They like to deal with differences directly and tend to "lay their cards on the table" in order to resolve issues.

■ *Contracts*

Americans are legalistic and like detailed contracts with all contingencies spelled out. These contracts tend to be fairly inflexible and are expected to be adhered to.

Mexico

■ *Relationship oriented*

It can take awhile to get to the serious content of a negotiation because Mexicans like to build rapport and a sense of friendship first. They like to build a solid relationship that they feel will last.

Many Mexicans feel that Americans have often taken advantage of them in the past and they may enter negotiations from a defensive position. They would like negotiations to proceed from a win/win attitude. It is important to stress friendship and a sense that both parties can win.

■ *Very expressive*

Mexicans can become very passionate during negotiations and express their feelings very openly and loudly. They do not mean anything personal; it is just their way of expressing themselves.

■ *Contracts*

Mexicans tend to dislike very detailed contracts. They see a contract as something to be strived for rather than a binding obligation. Their contracts are more likely to contain lofty principles than concrete details.

Negotiating

United States

■ *Dislike haggling*

Americans tend to be very competitive and want to get the best deal. However, the do very little haggling. Negotiating is usually a matter of finalizing the price and settling the details. Americans do not usually anticipate long-term negotiations. They believe in compromise and they believe there are universal rules of competition and fair play.

■ *Like formal agendas*

Americans like formal agendas for negotiating sessions and expect these agendas to be adhered to. They like fast-paced negotiations. Americans are very devoted to schedules, timelines and deadlines.

■ *Enjoy haggling*

Mexicans enjoy haggling; they feel that to take the first price is foolish. However, when you submit a proposal to them, don't inflate the price too much. They want bargaining to be enjoyable and the participants shouldn't take themselves too seriously. They like people to be assertive but will take their time making decisions until they trust you. Many times a meeting will conclude with "We'll let you know." This probably means the decision maker wasn't at the meeting.

Agreements often start with an oral agreement and then are followed by a written contract.

■ *Dislike formal agendas*

Mexicans tend to take a much more informal attitude toward negotiations. Agendas are more loose, and informal meetings are more important than formal ones. This reflects their view that establishing a business relationship is a personal one and they want to take time to build a friendship.

Mexicans are more casual toward time than Americans and this includes negotiating meetings which can run late or even be cancelled at the last minute.

United States

■ *Summary*

Be very punctual. Americans are very time conscious but it is acceptable to be 10 to 15 minutes late.

Americans like to get down to business right away. They want negotiations to move quickly. They also like people to be direct and candid. Indirect answers may be mistaken for lack of confidence or insincerity.

Americans dislike making concessions and do so grudgingly. Any concessions they make will often not come until the end of negotiations.

Americans tend to have limited experience with other cultures. This can lead many Americans negotiators to become too concerned with the technical part of the negotiations and forget about building relationships with other people.

Americans tend to attack issues sequentially, resolving them one issue at a time. They are much less likely to link them together.

Mexico

■ *Summary*

Mexicans have a more casual attitude toward time and don't want to rush to conclude a deal. You may have to make more than one trip to Mexico to conclude a deal.

Mexicans like to take time to establish an atmosphere of trust and friendship before doing business.

Pay attention to the issue of "face." Embarrassing a potential Mexican business partner could be very costly.

Avoid discussing politics or telling Mexicans "how we do it in America."

Mexicans tend to link issues together; they may indicate that specific issues must be resolved before other issues can even be discussed.

U.S. Business Etiquette

- Be punctual. Americans are very time conscious. They also tend to conduct business at a fairly fast pace.

- A firm handshake and direct eye contact is the standard greeting.

- Direct eye contact is very important in business. Not making eye contact implies boredom or disinterest.

- Gift giving is not common. The United States has bribery laws which restrict the value of gifts which can be given.

- The United States is not particularly rank and status conscious. Titles are not used when addressing executives. Americans usually like to use first names very quickly. Informality tends to be equated with equality.

- Business meetings usually start with a formal agenda and tasks to be accomplished. There is usually very little small talk. Participants are expected to express their ideas openly; disagreement are common.

- If there is no one to introduce you at a business meeting, you may introduce yourself and present your card.

- Permission should be asked before smoking.

- It is common to discuss business over breakfast, lunch or dinner. Also, some business deals are still concluded on the golf course.

- Business dress is basically conservative but gets more informal the further west you go.

- Decision making is actually decentralized and dispersed among many individuals and groups. It is important to find out who has final authority. Decision making tends to be quick.

- Many women hold middle management positions in the United States and a steadily growing number are in top executive positions. The same courtesy and respect should be shown women as men in business. Special or traditional courtesies such as opening doors are not always appreciated by women executives.

- U.S. companies pride themselves on being efficient, purposeful, direct, single-minded and materialistic. The bottom line is very important.

Mexican Business Etiquette

- Since education, title and family background provide social status, they are very important to recognize and respect when dealing with Mexicans. Address people by their title.

- Etiquette and manners are considered a measure of breeding.

- Dress and grooming are status symbols. Be conservative.

- Formality is preferred. Avoid the use of first names until a relationship has been established. Titles are important and Mexicans will expect you to use them in forms of address.

- Scheduling of appointments well in advance is highly recommended.

- When making small talk, avoid discussing illegal immigration or local poverty. Discussing children, family, soccer or Mexican culture is acceptable.

- Gift giving is not customary in social situations, but the gesture is appreciated. If you send flowers, yellow and purple are colors that connote death and should be avoided.

- Translate your business cards into Spanish. If you receive a letter in Spanish, reply in Spanish. There are a number of consulting companies that specialize in providing business translations.

- Many Mexicans have hyphenated names (i.e., Garcia-Lopez). The first name (Garcia) is the father's name and the second name (Lopez) is the mother's name. It is most common to address a person by both names, but if a name is shortened, it should be the father's name which is used.

- Entertainment is very important when doing business with Mexicans but business is usually not discussed. It purpose is to build a good business relationship.

U.S. Gestures

- Americans generally respect queues or lines. To shove or push one's way into a line will often result in anger and verbal complaint.

- Beckoning is done by raising the index finger and curling it in and out, or by raising the hand and curling the fingers back toward the body.

- Using the hand and index finger to point at objects or to point directions is common.

- Whistling is a common way to get the attention of someone at a distance.

- No is signalled by waving the forearm and hand (palm out) in front and across the upper body, back and forth.

- Americans use the standard OK sign, the V for victory sign and the thumbs up sign.

- Physical contact between members of the same sex is the norm. Close friends may even embrace.

- Mexicans stand closer to one another when talking than do North Americans.

- Mexicans tend to use the whole body when talking. They touch often.

- Mexicans also use lots of hand gestures.

- Placing your hands in your pockets is considered impolite in Mexico.

- It is customary in Mexico to shake hands when arriving and departing.

- Standing with your hands on your hips is considered challenging.

Communication Interferences

Effective communication, both verbal and nonverbal, means that the sending and processing of information between people, countries and businesses is understood, examined, interpreted, and responded to in some way. Any factor that causes a barrier or eliminates the successful transmission of information is defined as a communication interference.

- **Environmental interference** is an actual physical disturbance in the environment such as power outage, unregulated temperatures, a person or group talking very loud, etc.

- **Physiological interference** can be a hearing loss, laryngitis, illness, stuttering, neurological or organic deficit, etc.

- **Semantic interference.** We understand a word to have a certain meaning but the other person has a different meaning. Body language and gestures mean different things to different people. This includes confusion of abbreviated organizational jargon and pronunciation. Universal meanings (semantic understanding) are rare.

- **Syntactic interference.** Words are placed in certain order to give our language meaning. If the words are out of order, the meaning may be changed (this includes grammar).

- **Organizational interference.** Ideas being discussed lack sequence and can't be followed.

- **Psychological interference.** Words that incite emotion are used. In any emotional state (positive or negative) emotions need to be diffused in order to communicate effectively.

- **Social interference.** This includes cultural manners that are inappropriate for the country such as accepted codes for dress, business etiquette, communication rules, social activity.

Always become well informed about the customs and culture and get information before you try and do business in another country. Review this book and decide which areas of communication you and your colleagues will have difficulty with in Mexico. Anticipate and plan accordingly.

As the visitor to another country, you need to move out of your "comfort zone." Make the people from another country feel comfortable doing business with you.

No one country has a lock on world markets. Fundamental changes have occurred in the world economy in the last decade. New technologies and low labor costs often give nations that once were not major players an advantage. This results in increased competition. Yet international business is vital to any country's prosperity.

Business is conducted by people and the future of any country in a global economy will lie with people who can effectively think and act across ethnic, cultural and language barriers. We need to understand that the differences between nations and cultures is profound. The European-based culture of the United States has very different values and behaviors than other cultures in the world. If you cannot accept and adapt to these differences, you will not succeed.

Companies striving to market their business overseas can become truly successful only when they recognize that the key is operating with sensitivity toward the culture and communication of the other country. Communication cannot be separated from culture and this is true when doing business in other countries.

No flourishing company would present themselves to another company in the same country without researching that company's business culture and then adapting their image to meet the customer's comfort level. It's the same when doing business in another country. You must adapt your image by using your knowledge of effective cultural communication to present a positive public image to the other country.

The first thing is to identify your target audience: clients, customers, suppliers, financial people, government employees and so on. Then you must learn how to effectively communicate with them, and this means learning the culture.

Business failure internationally rarely results from technical or professional incompetence. It is often due to a lack of understanding of what people from other countries want, how they work and so on. This lack of understanding can put a company at a tremendous disadvantage.

Learning the business protocol and practices of the country where you want to do business can give you great leverage. The more you know about the people you do business with, the more successful you can be. Businesspeople need to make every contact they have with a foreign customer or business partner a positive one. Business leaders and managers must rethink the way they do business in the new global marketplace.

To be successful in the global market, you must:

- **Be flexible.** Adapting to differences in culture is necessary for individuals from both countries to get along and do business. Resisting the local culture will only lead to distrust.

- **Have patience.** Adjust your planning. Initiating business in many countries takes a long-range approach and may require two or three years. Anticipate problems and develop alternative strategies.

- **Prepare thoroughly.** Research the country, the organization, the culture and beliefs of the people you will be dealing with.

- **Know your bottom line.** Know exactly what you want from a deal and at what point an agreement is not in your best interest. Know when to walk away.

- **Show respect.** Search for the other side's needs and interests. Accentuate the positive. Don't preach your own beliefs, and respect their beliefs.

- **Form relationships.** Encourage getting involved with the new community if you are going to be in the country for a long period.

■ **Keep your cool.** Pay attention to the wide range of national, cultural, religious and social differences you encounter.

When you are using this book, review your own beliefs and values about correct business protocol and ethics. Then match these ideas with the business practices and protocol in Mexico.

You can contribute to your own success by recognizing that you will have to move out of your own "comfort zone" of doing business into the cultural business zone of Mexico in order to develop the rapport necessary to meet the needs of your client or partner. This does not mean you compromise your company's image or product but that you do business following Mexico's protocol while there. It's only for a short time that you may be following their rules, and the payoff can be one in which concepts can be sold while still maintaining a consistent image and approach that is culturally appropriate.

Quick Tips: United States

- The United States is a very ethnically diverse country. To do business with Americans, it is important to be open to this diversity and to be flexible.

- Americans tend to be very individually oriented and concerned with their own careers. Their first loyalty is to themselves.

- Americans want to be liked. The prefer people who are good team players and want to cooperate.

- Americans value equality and dislike people who are too status or rank conscious.

- Most Americans are open, friendly, casual and informal in their manners. They like to call people by first name quickly.

- Americans like to come right to the point and are uncomfortable with people who are indirect and subtle.

- Americans expect people to speak up and give their opinion freely and to be honest in the information they give. They like a direct and specific "yes" or "no."

- Americans can be very persistent. When they conclude a business transaction and sign a contract, they expect it to be honored. They do not like people who change their minds later.

Quick Tips: Mexico

- Personal relations are valued over business organizations. Learn to know and respect the people you work with and establish relationships with them.

- The Mexican business environment is more relaxed than in the U.S. Learn to adjust to their unhurried pace. It may take months to conclude a business deal. And be flexible with your deadlines.

- It is not necessary to be fluent in Spanish but it would be a good idea to learn some of the language. Significant business transactions may hinge on the Mexican perceptions of your commitment to them and learning the language helps. And remember that not all Spanish is alike. For example, do not use an interpreter from another Spanish speaking country.

- When negotiating in Mexico, keep things impersonal. Remember that respect means more to Mexicans than money.

- Mexican business and government are a tightly knit community. If you offend someone, the word will get around and hurt your business chances elsewhere.

Quick Tips: Mexico

■ While the Mexican business community is very
  male dominated, Mexicans have learned to deal
  with businesswomen from the United States
  Women will be respected and listened to as long
  as they can demonstrate their competence.

■ When negotiating with Mexicans, look for a fair
  deal; do not gouge. Don't put all your cards on
  the table as Mexicans like to bargain. Use
  silence effectively; do not rush to talk.
  Increased physical contact is often sign of
  progress.

■ Make sure you secure a written contract defining
  all the terms of your agreement. Mexicans can
  be very legalistic.

■ Companies considering moving to Mexico
  should consider some of the hidden costs of
  doing business there. These include: rate of
  productivity, worker training needed, cost of
  shipping, value of the peso, Mexican tax rates,
  and the amount of government control over
  labor benefits and environmental production.
  Also look at rates of economic growth in
  Mexico, rate of inflation and consumer spend-
  ing before deciding whether to locate there.
  These are as important as the lower wages given
  to Mexican workers.

- Worker incentives are very different in Mexico. Mexican workers are not workaholics like Americans and they tend not to be as interested in money. Therefore incentives that stress material benefits may not work.

- Above all, show respect for Mexicans and their culture. They want to feel they are being treated fairly.

Good morning	Buenas dias
Good afternoon	Buenas tardes
Good evening	Buenas noches
My name is...	My llamo...
What's your name?	Como se llama usted?
I'm pleased to meet you	Encantado de conocerle
How are you?	Como esta usted?
Fine, thank you	Bien, gracias
You're welcome	De nada
Excuse me	Perdon
Thank you	Muchas gracias
Yes/No	Si/No
Goodbye	Adios
Mr/Mrs/Miss	Senor/Senora/Senorita
See you again	Hasta la vista

Available in this series:

Business China

Business France

Business Germany

Business Japan

Business Mexico

Business Taiwan

For more information, please contact:

Sales and Marketing Department
NTC Publishing Group
4255 West Touhy Avenue
Lincolnwood, IL 60646
708-679-5500